Eggs, Toast, and Orange Juice

A Writer's Pocket Companion

Joy A. Burke

Copyright © 2019 by Joy A. Burke

All rights reserved. This book or any portion thereof may not be reproduced or used in any manner whatsoever without the express written permission of the publisher except for the use of brief quotations in a book review.

Printed in the United States of America
by Crooked Tail Press

First Printing, 2019

ISBN: 978-1-946380-12-8

CROOKED TAIL PRESS
www.crookedtailpress.com

Table of Contents

Introduction	p. 11
Semper Paratus	p. 17
10 Quick Tips About Writing	p. 23
An Introduction to the Present	p. 31
Being a Writer Series 1.1	p. 37
Being a Writer Series 1.2	p. 47
Being a Writer Series 1.3	p. 57
Invisible Fences	p. 65
Is Writer's Block Real?	p. 71
It's Okay to Make Faces	p. 77
Opportunities as Writers	p. 83
Eggs, Toast, and Orange Juice	p. 91
Canvas of Creation	p. 97
About the Author	p. 103

For Gloria, Amy, Mary, and Maya.

Thank you for being you,
and always encouraging me to be me.

You are the greatest dream champions.

INTRODUCTION

Writing is a lonely job.

It sure seems romantic and like a great idea when you start out. All those plots and all that passion just bursting at the seam. But at some point, you realize it can be very lonely and is almost always exceptionally quiet.

We all talk to ourselves – that's sort of what we do as writers. But, occasionally, we don't have the answers to our own questions. Or, how about this: we think about them so much we confuse the right answer with all the various possibilities. So, what's a writer to do?

Well, there's lots of options including joining a writer's group or an online writing community. Both are good options. But sometimes, we don't have the courage or the confidence. Our writing is like our children! We really don't want to let them out into the world until we're ready.

When I was coordinator of a regional writer's organization, I developed a newsletter that spoke to being a writer every day. How we live and breathe being a writer while being a spouse, a parent, a business owner, and so many other things we writers are.

When my time as coordinator came to a close, I was asked by many of the members to compile a book of the articles from the newsletter. Very few changes have been made, and you'll find salutations included as they were in the original article. I have however, added some content in the form of action items or additional resources following each entry. At the time of this writing, all links and reference to articles and resources are current and useable. You will see a reference or two to my early blog/website – this is an old space given no attention which I leave up for references such as this. Please give a once-young writer and blogger grace as you peruse the site.

So, a few years late, here it is. A small writer's handbook of encouragement, ideas, and principles.

We are all on a journey where our words can shape our futures. I wish you the most wonderful journey knowing you can create an amazing future.

Happy Writing,

Joy Burke

Eggs, Toast, and Orange Juice

A Writer's Pocket Companion

Semper Paratus

Always Prepared. Are you?

My husband bought new boots for work yesterday. If you don't know, he's a garbage truck driver, or 'sanitation technician.' These boots are advertised as the most comfortable, most durable, and guaranteed waterproof. The perfect boot for any condition. Given his profession, you can imagine the hunt for such a boot is constant. He picked up a pair, came home, laced 'em up, and took them around the house for a spin. All was well and he was a happy camper for the hour or two test drive.

This morning, about 7:30, only an hour and a half into his route, he texts me asking if I can bring him his old pair. His feet are killing him. I ran out and grabbed the old, rugged, tattered, sad looking pair that today, were his salvation.

I am so thankful I was home so I could bring those boots to him. One of the many things I love about my husband is his ability to improvise and push through hard times. If I weren't home, he would have worked just as hard, and finished on time - as always. It made me wonder about my own preparedness. How well am I really equipped to write when conditions aren't favorable? Today, for example, my entire routine was thrown off and I didn't adjust to get in my free writing time. If it were Shawn (hubby), it would've gotten done.

How prepared and flexible are you?

Well, the hunt for the ideal boot continues. And the effort to maintain a writing schedule despite distractions and interruptions will double. In the meantime, I'm going to go get a cookie…

Have a warm, stay-out-of-the-rain weekend.

JB

• Questions to Consider •

Our brains, like every other muscle in the body, need training to know what we want it to do. We've all heard of 'muscle memory' – that same principle can be applied to our brains, if we exercise and train it.

The best way to strengthen and train the muscles in your writing brain is to use them. Doing so provides your brain the tools it needs to perform under pressure. That's why creating a writing routine – and sticking to it – is so important.

With that in mind, reflect on your writing habits as you read the following questions.

1. What is your writing routine? Do you have one?

   ----

2. How does your writing routine allow for flexibility?

----

3. How do you equip yourself to write on the fly, in situations you didn't know you'd find yourself in?

----

4. If you don't have a writing routine, why not start one now?

----

5. What do you feel is your biggest distraction from writing? What can you do to help minimize it?

• Notes & Ideas •

Joy A. Burke

• Notes & Ideas •

10 Quick Tips About Writing

Everyone wants to sound like they know what they're talking about. The same goes for writing.

Whether you are a student, an aspiring author, a professional in a workplace, or a business owner, when you are submitting something others will read, you want to sound competent and articulate.

Here are some quick tips to get you started that are surprisingly overlooked.

1. Hook the reader.

It doesn't matter what you are writing, or who you are writing it for, if you don't grab the reader's attention straight away you may as well have not written the piece. Your headline, title, and first line are the best places to do this.

2. Create an engaging piece.

Once you've hooked the reader, you better deliver on your 'promise'. They are now expecting you to follow through on your great title or opening line. You came up with it, go ahead and continue your thought through to the end and dazzle your readers. Use facts, humor (sparingly), anecdotes, or in the case of a story – a great plot and character development.

3. Get personal.

Opening yourself up to your reader is an excellent way to keep them engaged. We all like to feel we are being entrusted with special or personal information. This doesn't always mean you have to employ the use of personal pronouns. It could be as simple as the subject matter you chose to write about and the way in which you write it. If it's a novel or short story, it could be your point of view or homing in on a specific incident 'behind closed doors' that characters in the rest of the story are not privy to.

4. Make it grammatically correct.

This one may surprise you, but don't let your guard down. With the advent of spell check and auto correct, most people become pretty relaxed about their spelling and grammar. Don't let that be you. Submit polished pieces regardless if you are having a friend proofread or you are sending off to an editor. *You* are the first line of defense for your piece.

5. Use quotes whenever possible.

This includes press releases and articles. The more you bring your reader in with real experiences from other people, the more interested they will be in experiencing it for themselves. How often do we think, 'Well, that's *their* opinion. Would my experience be the same? Would I feel the same way?' Quoting is not to challenge that person's experience or expertise, it is simply used to encourage others to get out and experience it (whatever *it* is) for themselves. And of course, in the case of novels or stories, quoting – or dialogue – is essential for pacing and story development. It brings characters alive and gives them personalities and brings voice to their struggles and triumphs.

6. Use sensory imagery.

Our most powerful sense is our sense of smell. It lingers longest and brings back the most potent memories. Utilizing all the senses when describing story scenes, products, and services (if scent applies to your business) is always a great idea; however, our sense of smell goes the furthest with the fewest words. But be advised, smells evoke different *emotions* for everyone, and they can be general. If I write 'smelled like flowers' hundreds of smells can come to mind. But if I write 'smelled like my grandmother's garden full of gardenias', it's much more specific what I'm smelling.

7. Include a list.

This is most effective in non-fiction writing. Lists help people compartmentalize, read quickly and clearly, and prioritize. See how often lists are used in top stories and headlines next time you read the news. This method is still used in fiction – usually in children's books when the protagonist is checking off what he or she has to do for school, or what the young detective has deduced so far, etc. which brings the reader along on the journey.

8. Check your structure.

This has a lot to do with whether or not your piece is readable and if the order make sense. Does your third paragraph sound more like the opening than your first paragraph does? Does your last paragraph leave your reader hanging? Sometimes it's helpful to print out your piece, number each paragraph, then cut up the piece by paragraph and move them around on a desk until you find an order – a structure – that flows well and reads naturally.

9. Cut unnecessary words.

There are almost always extra words. By nature, most of us write like we talk. This is not necessarily a bad thing, but it can take up valuable space in people's brains as they read and most certainly on the page. Common culprits: that, could, would, he, she, they, it, very, up. The best way to cut words: write the piece, shelve it a day or two, print it, re-read it, and I can almost guarantee you'll find things to reword or cut. It can also be beneficial to read your piece out loud to see what doesn't fit.

10. Provide insight.

Above all, you want whatever it is you are writing to shed light on the topic you are writing about. There is no need to preach, simply share in a way that is enriching and helps others grow.

• Questions to Consider •

1. Pull out your last piece and look at it with fresh eyes. Based on the first few sentences, would you be interested in reading more if you hadn't written it?

   ---

2. Write memos often? Next time you do, or any other sort of interoffice communication, write using at least a few of the earlier points. How did people respond? Did you get a more engaged audience?

   ---

3. As a creative writer, hooking the reader is imperative. Take a look at a few of your favorite books. What hooks you about how this author writes or how the story begins?

   ---

4. Now, review some of your own writing. Be honest with yourself: how well do you hook the reader?

• Notes & Ideas •

• Notes & Ideas •

An Introduction to the Present...

It can be easy to get caught up in our to-do lists, emails, and the latest social media craze only to completely forget what we had for breakfast. Sound familiar to anyone else? Well, that's completely me! The only reason I know I've had Multi-Grain Cheerios for breakfast today is because I'm eating as I type.

On Tuesday, I enjoyed tea with my dear friend and published author, Maya Sullivan (http://www.daretobeyourownboss.net). One of the important things we talked about was living in the present (which means knowing you ate your Cheerios without having to watch yourself do it!) when most of us are busy making our to-do lists for the day. I couldn't help but admit I had an 8.5 x 11 sheet of paper outlining my tasks for the day, but that was her point. If we all keep bustling around working hard toward *that* success over there, we will never enjoy *this* success right here that we're living in! And believe me, you *are* living in a success. It may not be the success you dreamed you'd be in right now, but right now, wherever you are, you are in success! So enjoy it!

What is success? And how do we live in the present to accept and enjoy it?

Success can be typing those 25 words you didn't yesterday. It can be writing a blog post! For yourself, or someone else. It can be mustering up the courage to write an email asking to guest post, teach a class, send your book in as a potential learning tool, write a query, spending ten minutes listing potential agents to contact. Success comes in massively different forms for each of. Take a moment right now and identify what success you can eat a chocolate for! And don't forget to savor it.

As writers – and you are a writer – there is always something to be doing, even aside from actually *writing*. So, over the next few weeks, in a handful of short articles like this one, we're going highlight a few of the basics of being a writer, if your goal is to write professionally. The topics will vary and they may not apply to each of you, but hopefully, you can pass it on to someone else.

Wishing each of you a beautiful day living in the present, and hoping you cultivate the art of identifying and celebrating successes!

Write Happy,

JB

• Questions to Consider •

1. What is your definition of success?

   _____

   _____

   _____

2. How well do you live in the present? What can you do to help yourself enjoy and savor the moment you're living?

   _____

   _____

   _____

3. What does it mean to be a writer *to you*?

   _____

   _____

   _____

4. Moving forward, how are you going to combine success in your life as a writer?

_____

_____

_____

• Notes & Ideas •

• Notes & Ideas •

Being a Writer Series 1.1

Being a writer means you're in business. Mostly. Depends on what type of writer you are. Many people view writers as falling into four categories:

1. Hobbyists/recreational – enjoy writing, but don't go much beyond writing for friends or locally.
2. Professional – working for another company (magazines/newspapers, editor, technical...).
3. Freelancer – much like a professional, but is self-employed. This terms often has a negative connotation associated with it.
4. Professionally published author – as in books on the shelves at your local store.

So, before you decide much more about anything regarding your writing life – meaning should you publish, what should you write/to what market, can I make a career out of this, etc. – you should determine which category of writer you fall into.

If decide you're content writing for pleasure and have no intent of monetizing your writing, you're good-to-go. No need to worry about a business or marketing plan, or establishing the connections that will build your platform and make sales. But, if you fall into categories 2-4, you are running a business.

So, what does that mean?

It means a mentality shift, for many. Just about any writer I've ever known who works for anyone else, also is writing for themselves on the side. So, while they may fall into category #2, they also are in categories #3 & 4 as well. This means it really is time to sit down and ask yourself 'What is my plan? What are my goals? And how am I going to get there?'

While the market and audience targeting will be slightly different for technical writers than it is for children's authors, the principles and planning stages are the same: you need to have them for success (generally speaking – there are of course those lucky stars!).

How do you do it?

Once you determine your goals for your career, find the resources to help you get there. Resources can include:

- A support network: friends, family, other writers and professionals.
- A mentor: someone who has gone on this journey and is a little further along and can offer advice.
- Classes and workshops: not just writing classes, but business and marketing classes, classes on social media, speaking, networking, business building etc. All these elements will contribute to your success.

- - These can be in-person and online. Lots of opportunities.
- Books, seminars, videos, webinars, etc. Any medium you feel you can glean answers from.

Feel a little much simply to write a book?

Maybe.

But consider this:

If you want a successful book launch, how will you achieve that if you've been tucked away writing for months or years and made no connections? And how do you plan to manage the publicity, monies, further writing offers if you do not have the people and PR skills needed to handle the pressure, let alone the bookkeeping abilities to manage the financial end of the spectrum. Are you already equipped to hire someone to set you up and maintain your records?

This article is not an attempt to overwhelm or discourage you! It is an attempt to help you realize (if you don't already!) that writing is in fact a business. Just like charities are. All the same components apply.

So, to *avoid* overwhelm during the process, *prepare* for it now.

Some of my personal favorite resources which are helpful and inspirational (mix of writing, business, & marketing):

- On Writing Well – William Zinsser

- The Well-Fed Writer – Peter Bowerman
- Secrets of a Freelance Writer – Bob Bly
- Inbound Marketing – Brian Halligan | Dharmesh Shah
- The Wealthy Freelancer – Steve Slaunwhite, Pete Savage, Ed Gandia
- http://thewritepractice.com/ - Website devoted to writers becoming better *through practice*. Established and run by Joe Bunting.
- https://mirasee.com/ - Established and run by Danny Iny. (Used to be known as Firepole Marketing) FYI, while content is usually interesting – *lots* of emails. Can manage preference and get a weekly digest.
- http://www.thebookdesigner.com/ - Doesn't just address designing books. All sorts of great stuff! Joel Friedlander.

• Questions to Consider •

1. Re-read the four category types of writers. What type of writer are you? What type of writer do you *want* to be?

---

2. If you're content with where you're at – awesome! But, if you want more, what will it take for you to get it? What will you need to implement/change/rethink for you to become the writer you want to be?

---

3. Who are you writing for? Do they know it? What are a few ideas you can implement soon to reach them?

_____

_____

_____

_____

_____

_____

4. What are your goals for your writing life?

_____

_____

_____

_____

_____

_____

_____

5. What resources are you taking advantage of to reach those goals?

_____

_____

_____

6. What resources are you going to add to help reach your goals?

_____

_____

_____

_____

_____

_____

7. Write out the next three steps you will take to define your writing life and reach your goals:

_____

_____

_____

Joy A. Burke

• Notes & Ideas •

• Notes & Ideas •

Being a Writer Series 1.2

Let's delve a little deeper, shall we?

Last time, we spoke about writing being a business. For many it's a mentality shift. The romantic notion of a writer tucked away in a cabin in the woods, typing away while sipping coffee – is mostly for the big screen.

The reality is *most* of us check our bank accounts daily to see if anyone has purchased our $.99 ebook we slaved over for two years and are now practically giving away. We can't afford that cabin in the woods.

Which brings me to my next topic.

It's timely and touchy but because it keeps popping up for me, I feel it's part of what I need to share. It may not apply to all of you, but I think it will apply to many. And full disclaimer: this one's a bit longer...

Without authors there are no books. So why should any of us feel we can't or shouldn't or don't deserve or feel qualified to be paid for or writing (or worth!)?

If you had the good fortune to hear Bernadette Pajer speak last Saturday she mentioned this as well. Briefly, but I would like to touch on it a little more in earnest. Because if you plan to make a career out of writing, you need to get paid for your books, articles, or time. Not piecemeal it out in pennies.

As an overall collective of women, and the entirety of us comprised of thoughtful, compassionate individuals, it's in our nature to give, share, and educate. But even Mother Theresa didn't make her way in this world on generosity alone. She had to work for it and market. She brought her passion and mission to the forefront of the world, got them on board so she could do what she loved. We need to do that, too. It's difficult, but important.

When we write, we impart a little of ourselves with every word: our knowledge, our hearts, our experiences, and our histories. As a whole, this is priceless and contributes to the intellectual value of our culture.

If you spend time and money investing in your craft, growing, cultivating your skills, and evolving to be a better writer than you were 100 pages ago, a year ago – you deserve every penny you charge for your work. So, show it in how you price your product. Because that's what it is: a product. Yes, it may be a literary masterpiece, but it's also a product that goes on a shelf and people often value *products* by their price.

A side note on the psychology of price: people value more and invest more when they have to pay for it. The more they pay for it the more they are willing to invest in it. And if you can create headlines and jacket information that pull your readers in enough and tells them *the irresistible benefits* of reading your book (the mystery they've been waiting for, the heroine they've wanted to read about, the cooking book finally addressing turnips), they'll pay for it.

You are an author. And should be treated as such and with the same respect as anyone else whose name is in print. Don't deny yourself this honor and right. You've worked hard for it!

Most of us doubt our natural abilities. I get that. But don't. However, if you are part of this group, *you are a writer*. And you're only going to get better.

Charging your worth – or even at all – can be yet another mindset shift. But it's worth it. If you're still hesitant or not sure which steps to take, here are a few to consider:

1. Look in the mirror and say, 'I *am* a writer.'
2. Believe that you are.
3. Repeat until you do.
4. If you are giving your work away for free, please stop. If you feel you must, limit yourself to providing a chapter or two for free to tease them into purchasing your entire book!
5. Set reasonable prices for your books or products.
    a. Consider having multiple price points for people to try you out before they invest $20+ dollars.
    b. This would be where a $.99 or $2.99 ebook would be appropriate.

6. *Do your research.* The average ebook, including best-sellers, *sell* from $3-$9. Most ebooks are *priced* around $.99-$3.99. Where does yours fit in? Food for thought.
7. It's okay to fiddle with your prices! You won't know what your particular market will pay unless you do. No one expects you to get it up there with the golden price the first time. But that's the beauty of our era in publishing, isn't it? The massive flexibility! So, experiment.
8. A book won't sell if no one knows about it. So, get out there and *advertise*!

So go, price your books what *you're* worth, and what you want, and show the world what they've been missing!

JB

Here are a couple links you may be interested in for a little extra reading.

https://gigaom.com/2013/05/30/free-is-not-the-magic-number-new-trends-in-ebook-pricing/

https://www.idealog.com/blog/changing-book-business-seems-flowing-downhill-amazon/

https://www.writtenwordmedia.com/2018/01/08/publishing-trends-indie-publishing/

• Questions to Consider •

1. Do you believe you're a writer? Do others? When you say 'I'm a writer/author' do you hope no one will look you up and discover you've not published?

   ----

2. Why do you think so many writers believe no one will buy their work? Do you believe that? Why?

   ----

3. If you have a book or ebook published, how are your sales? Is it priced where you want it? If not, why?

4. Spend some time doing a little market research. What is the average price for a print and ebook in your niche? Where will you price yours?

5. What actions can/will you take to grow yourself as a writer and develop your craft? Do you think that will help you make the mental shift in pricing or marketing?

---

6. If you aren't selling copies of your book, and your goal is to write for a career, what can you do differently?

---

7. What stuck out to you most about this chapter? Why?

---

8. What are the next two steps you plan to take?

• Notes & Ideas •

• Notes & Ideas •

Being a Writer Series 1.3

Establishing Habits for Success

If you saw my blog post about my cat Toby's eating habits, you'll know where I stand on creating healthy habits. If not, feel free to link over, but here it is in sum:

Your brain, like any other muscle in your body, needs to be worked out. So, train it! Get it in shape to the point where if you're *not* writing, it's asking you why.

But that's not the only healthy habit writers should be entertaining. Here are the top five habits I personally feel writers who are freelancers or on their way to publishing should be practicing, and why:

Write Regularly

I don't need to elaborate much on this one since I just spoke on it. If you'd like more, you may read my blog post here: http://www.hahaink.com/tobys-process/

Stay Up-to-Date in the Writing World

If you don't know what's selling and how, who's reading what, who's published what, what editors are open to new authors, and what those editors accept, that puts you at the back of the line.

Cruise Twitter for two minutes and you'll find a dozen or more vampire pararomance writers. There's not an editor that will go near it right now – the market is saturated with it. Give it another five to eight years and they'll be gobbling it up, no doubt. But not now. So, pay attention.

Socialize / Network

Writing by its very nature is solitary work. We need to get out or the only people we'll be talking to are the ones in our heads! And we know what they do to people like that...

This is often a great way to stay in the know, brainstorm, develop as a writer, learn, develop relationships, and is usually a safe place to workshop your writing. Do not underestimate the power of relationships. We all need other trusted writers to review our work and spur us on.

You don't have to limit your socializing/networking to writers, either. Joining the local chamber of commerce or networking groups can be just as effective in establishing connections and growing relationships. Remember, word of mouth is the most powerful marketing there is – no matter if it comes from a business owner or another writer.

Invest in Your Craft

I am pleased I can look back at my writing in high school and college and say 'Wow, that's pretty good!' But I'm *relieved* I can look at it now and say, 'This is better.' If I can't do the same in another year, two, or three, then I have failed myself and anyone who has invested money or time in my work, simply because I have decided I've become the best I can be. Not so! We can *always* learn more. And you should make every attempt to. Whether that be in the form of continuing education classes, online education, workshops, or diligently attending writer's groups and conferences. It all matters!

If we become complacent as writers, not 'exercising' our brains and tending to them, how on earth can we expect people to love us or our characters when neither are growing?

Receive Criticism

This of course is one of the hardest things to do in all areas of our lives. But, what I feel is one of the most important and why it is on the list. I am not suggesting you accept all criticism – especially if your gut tells you it's against the nature of your character or even your own. But it's important to consider those who you've allowed to read your work as your potential audience...that you could be writing *to them*. So, what they have to share may really help your piece or provide insight into how you could craft it slightly different.

Even if you don't take someone's suggestion verbatim, listening to their criticism – hopefully constructive and not negative – may spark that idea that's been evading you for weeks!

Taking notes on what people have to say often helps, since few of us ever do well under pressure. That way, you can come back to it when it's not so raw, review the suggestions, and see if any will strengthen your story.

That's it! Those are my personal top five habits writers should practice for healthy writing. I hope you've found something useful and are motivated to jump back into that story you've been avoiding.

Happy Writing!

JB

• Questions to Consider •

1. What habits do you currently have in place for your writing?

   ----

2. Of the five suggested habits listed above, which might be the hardest to incorporate into your routine? Why?

_____

_____

3. How do you currently socialize? It's not only important for our mental health as writers, but as mentioned earlier, for the success of our writing. If you don't spend time networking or socializing, spend some time finding what groups are available in your area. List them here for future reference.

_____

_____

_____

_____

_____

_____

_____

_____

_____

Eggs, Toast, and Orange Juice

• Notes & Ideas •

• Notes & Ideas •

Invisible Fences

Create Enforceable Boundaries

How was your Independence Day? I hope it was relaxing, full of color and time with the people you enjoy. Many people opt to head out of town for the holiday, to take a little vacation. Did you?

As writer's it can be hard to get away. Sure, we might *physically* step away from our desks, but are you able to take your mind away from the task at hand? Whether it be the novel you're working on, or the article your writing, we can get so involved in our work we forget to set healthy boundaries.

Maybe you don't have this problem and it's just me but, bear with me a moment.

I'm constantly thinking about what I'm working on, and if I'm not currently working on a project I'm wondering what I could start. This often leaves me mentally exhausted. And leaves nothing or very little left for my family, and when I am with them, I'm often distracted because I'm thinking. Who, exactly, is benefiting from this mentality? No one, really. Yet, while I see it, I can't seem to break the pattern.

So, this is where we all need to recognize in ourselves where we need to erect our invisible fences. It's important to give your all to your work – during work hours. But it's just as important, maybe more so, to give your family, friends, pets, home – whatever – your all during your non-work hours. It will keep your mind and body healthy and refreshed, and provide that mini-vacation from the swirl of words we're constantly up against.

So, here's my action plan, yours too if you want it:

1. Write out the projects that need to be completed, with completion dates.
2. Establish hours of each day I will work.
3. Pen in break times, and no-work times (like weekends which I am *notorious* for working throughout).
4. During breaks and no-work times, take a short walk, do some deep breathing, and focus on anything other than writing! Get some physical activity.
5. Make a daily wrap-up sheet at the end of my work day so I know exactly what I've done and what I need to do so my mind has some closure and isn't thinking about it all evening or weekend.

It's a start. We'll see how it works!
Enjoy your mini-vacations this week.

Happy Writing,

JB

• Questions to Consider •

1. If you have them, how are your boundaries between writing and non-writing time? How do you actually *feel* during these times?

----

2. If you don't have boundaries, those set hours for writing, how do you think that would make a difference for you – for your family?

----

3. Moving forward, what tweaks can you make to your schedule or habits to include those invisible fences?

4. Will you adopt my schedule for boundaries or create one of your own? If you create your own, write it here:

• Notes & Ideas •

• Notes & Ideas •

Is Writer's Block Real?

Or is it something else...

I'm a fan of writer's block. It gives me all sorts of excuses to do other non-essential things like surf the internet for the cure, have a snack, and read. Okay, reading I can get away with because if I don't read, I don't grow. But still – stay focused, right?!

Personally, for me, I think writer's block is a synonym for procrastination, disinterest, and oftentimes fear. Regardless of the reasoning, I think it's safe to say we've all suffered from it at one point or another – so how to overcome it? There's no single answer. Countless articles and books have been written in an attempt to combat this great disease afflicting so many writers, but alas, we still suffer.

But here are a few ideas nonetheless. Some no doubt you are familiar with, some perhaps you read yourself this week, and maybe to some of you, there's something new in the batch. Hopefully, just reading about writer's block will get you moving again!

Take a walk – or other form of exercise. This one is the most effective for me. Nothing gets my creativity flowing like being outside and enjoying nature's bounty...or people watching!

Look at pictures – this is also effective for me as I'm a relatively visual person. It doesn't work for everyone, but I can't help but wonder what's just outside the frame of the picture, or what's lurking *inside* the castle; what caused the photographer to take the photo she did, or why the colors are just so...

Talk out your hurdles – often, talking with another creative about why we are stumped or where we are stumped can iron out or kinks and get us back on track, or head us in a new direction that is exciting and fresh.

Take cues from your dreams – a fun article from The Write Practice this week discussed how our dreams can get us moving again: http://thewritepractice.com/writers-block-dreams/?awt_l=FitjI&awt_m=3anLLqF0BGsKU5r

Article title: How to Overcome Writer's Block While You Sleep

Write something completely out of your genre – if you're a mystery writer, write something in the sci-fi or fantasy genre and vice versa; if you are a romance writer, try mystery or comedy. This really gets you thinking outside the box. Here's a fun activity you can even do with your kids (yes, I do this even for fun!): http://thewritepractice.com/story-game/?utm_source=feedburner&utm_medium=feed&utm_campaign=Feed%3A+TheWritePractice+%28The+Write+Practice%29

Article title: Let's Play a Story Game to Break Writer's Block

So, there you have it. A few easy to do and fun writer's block busters.

Wishing you a creative weekend,

JB

• Questions to Consider •

1. What do you do when you have writer's block?

   ----

2. Which of these ideas might you try next time writer's block makes an appearance?

• Notes & Ideas •

• Notes & Ideas •

It's Okay to Make Faces!

At least when you write...

You're in the middle of a scene, your character sees the woman he's loved all his life as he looks up from the newspaper he's reading at the local coffee shop. He just stares. He can't do anything else. She has a spell on him. But it's not just *any* stare - it's the stare of a man who's been in love with a woman he admires and respects, but who doesn't know he exists. But....what exactly does that stare look like? So, you find yourself practicing in front of your computer until your facial muscles tell you you've got it right. Sound familiar?

Or what about the villain who's about to make his move? Or a jealous friend, or someone who got the raw end of the deal - what do they look like? How are you going to *show* what they're felling rather than tell it? Through their facial features.

Then there's the character who endears himself to all readers: always has the best of intentions but always seems to bungle things up or throw a wrench in the plot just when things were going so well. And as he tries to make it better, it continues to spiral downward! What does he look like as he discovers each 'whoopsie?'

When I'm in the making faces stage of my writing - my cats tend to stay clear. I imagine they think I'm morphing into some strange creature and don't want to be around if they discover it preys on cats. But allowing yourself the freedom to get a little silly in your writing space brings your characters alive to your readers - and to you! Next time you cringe, maybe you'll remember how our accident-prone character above feels every time he intervenes - and just maybe you'll discover a way to make him the hero as you iron out your own features into a smile once again.

Happy Writing,

JB

• Questions to Consider •

1. How do you create your character expressions?

   ----

2. Has anyone ever walked by while you were making a face trying to capture the emotion of your character? Write that experience here!

   ----

3. If you haven't used faces to capture emotion in the past for your characters, consider it now. How do you think it will help the 'show-don't-tell' factor in your writing?

• Notes & Ideas •

• Notes & Ideas •

Opportunities as Writers

We write...what else?

Sometimes I sit behind my computer and get so focused on working I miss opportunities. What sort of opportunities? Let's see...

Meeting new people that could open doors for me or grow my contact base.

Nurturing relationships that could turn into referrals for work, book sales, or teaching opportunities.

Sharing what I know already and gaining authority and credibility in the circles I'm already a part of because I'm focusing on reaching out where no one knows me.

That's just to name a few. And this doesn't just apply to me - I have no doubt this applies to others as well. Sure, I work for businesses building websites, ghostwriting blogs/articles, and helping with email campaigns - but I also write fiction, enter contests, dream of publishing my own collection of shorts stories that people simply can't put down.

But, no one will know I exists or do any of these things if I don't get out from behind my computer and make the most of the opportunities that exist.

What that entails?

- ✓ Getting out of my comfort zone (= out of PJ's and potentially out of my house).
- ✓ Spending more time sharing what I already know and less time building a knowledge base and worrying about perfecting the presentation (this translates into regularly blogging, publishing articles on LinkedIn, teaching, writing coaching, etc.).
- ✓ Reaching out to acquaintances, friends, family, etc. to build stronger relationships and truly establish myself as a writer and professional in their eyes (this could mean something as simple as coffee or lunch to visit and catch up - easy enough to let people know what I've been up to and why. Great chance to articulate what I do. Or what about sending a card...). Then, when they hear of an opportunity, hopefully they think of me first.

Right now, I imagine people generally don't know what I do, and certainly wouldn't think of me if they heard of someone needing to write half a dozen articles or blog posts, but not having the time to get it done.

What could all this lead to in the end, not only as a business owner, but as a writer?

- ✓ Teaching

- ✓ Speaking
- ✓ Writing
- ✓ Writing Coaching
- ✓ Passive income from other products (workbooks, webinars, podcasts, tele-seminars, at-home courses etc.)
- ✓ Interviews

Opportunities are all around us. The possibilities are endless - but often, we have to look up enough to recognize they're there. And then, it's the scary step of taking advantage of them.

Wishing you a courageous weekend,

JB

• Questions to Consider •

1. What opportunities do you currently take advantage of let the world know you exist as a writer?

----

2. What opportunities are out there that you haven't taken advantage of that you've felt that nudging toward?

----

3. If you write for businesses or others, do people know what you do? If you write fiction do people know where they can get your books and why they should invest in you?

----

4. Have you thought about ways you, as a writer of any sort, can gain passive income from your skills? If so, in what ways?

_____

_____

_____

5. If not, would you consider it? As noted above, easy ways to do so are:
   a. Teaching
   b. Speaking
   c. Writing
   d. Coaching
   e. Passive income from other products (workbooks, webinars, podcasts, tele-seminars, at-home courses etc.)
   f. Interviews

   Which would you be willing to consider?

_____

_____

_____

_____

_____

_____

• Notes & Ideas •

• Notes & Ideas •

Eggs, Toast, and Orange Juice

When I was contemplating this week's piece for our Being a Writer series, I happened to be reading a post on writing devices from The Write Practice blog. It's here if you'd like to enjoy it as well.

<u>Article title:</u> Three Literary Devices You Should Be Using in Your Writing

As I was reading, I came across a few areas in punctuation that gave me pause. I know, so small in the large spectrum of things and no doubt I'm over thinking it…but…if I am, maybe others are as well. So, here's the scoop:

Commas: Do you use a comma in a series of three or more?

Commonly called the Oxford or Serial comma, this is a subject of *great* debate. **The answer:** Your preference. I personally feel a writer should include it, as it prevents any chance of misunderstanding. I like my eggs, toast, and OJ. I do not like my eggs, toast and OJ. Meaning to me, that the toast and OJ are one thing rather than two separate things as made clear with the additional comma. On the other hand, journalists in *Smithsonian* and *National Geographic* do not, and well – if only one day I could write for them...So what it boils down to is personal preference and, if you have one, your editor's style.

Periods: Inside or outside the quotation?

Talk about inconsistent! I am not immune either – every time I quote something or someone, I hesitate before closing the quote and placing the period (or comma). Where exactly does it go?

The answer: It depends on where you/your audience lives.

In American English, it's correct to put periods/commas *inside* the quotations. However, in British English, they can decide whether to put them inside or outside based on the rules of the sentence: does the punctuation go with the quote, or with the entire sentence? Much like we do with question marks and exclamation points.

So, I suppose if you make a mistake – just say your English!

Oh, and on that note: if you say you are English, you are from England. If you say you are British, you are from Great Britain which includes England, Scotland, and Wales. This too, is a common mistake.

I will sign off with those simple two for today. Perhaps you learned something, perhaps not, or perhaps you had some ideas solidified. Regardless, I hope you enjoyed the read and have a wonderful weekend.

Happy Writing,

JB

• Questions to Consider •

1. Has the Oxford comma debate ever been in question to you, or have you always known the correct placement?

   ----

2. As you read (and I know you read extensively), do you find yourself stumbling upon small grammatical issues like the Oxford comma? If so, do you take the time to look it up? Might you in the future?

   ----

3. What grammatical nuances cause you to stumble? Note them here and as you have time (or even now!) look up the appropriate use of each.
   TIP: Readers won't always know what's wrong grammatically, but they'll often be able to tell that

something is wrong. They'll often assume it's something with the story that made them unsettled and not grammar since they were unable to identify the problem. Help yourself and get your grammar right so your readers don't question the story.

• Notes & Ideas •

• Notes & Ideas •

Canvas of Creation

Isn't that just lovely?

There were many things that resonated with me Saturday when Bill Kenower came to speak (which was *amazing!!*), but for whatever reason, that continues to ring in my mind. *Canvas of Creation.*

Perhaps it's because it can mean something unique to each person who hears or reads it. What does it mean to you? What image does it conjure? Overall, for me, I have an overwhelming sense of *hope*.

Strange maybe, but as authors, a blank page is a fresh start. Sure, a little daunting, but at the same time, our imaginations are our only limitation! That's a lot of creating. And a lot of different canvases.

I don't know about you, but when I hear the word 'canvas' I immediately think color which leads me to think of unique. When I think 'creation' I immediately think great big world, which leads me then to think of imagination. Combined, that's great big colorful uniqueness from the imagination. And that's what we do isn't it? We create what others can't to provide color in this world.

Canvas of Creation.

Love it.

Have a colorful and creative weekend.

JB

• Questions to Consider •

1. How do you feel when you see a blank page? Is it daunting or does it feel like a fresh start? An opportunity to *create*?

   ----

2. What does 'Canvas of Creation' mean to you?

Joy A. Burke

• Notes & Ideas •

Eggs, Toast, and Orange Juice

• Notes & Ideas •

(*Me at Inspiration Point in Grand Teton National Park. I can't believe I made it!*)

Joy A. Burke is an award-winning short story writer and author of eight books. Her latest fiction book, 'Nora: Witch in Training' is a short sweet mystery for younger readers published in October 2019. She teaches creative writing to those who still dream and is a sought-after speaker on self-publishing for beginners.

When she and her husband aren't making their way through national or state parks, Joy lives in Washington State with her husband and four cats.

To learn more about Joy, get in touch, find out how she can help you achieve your writing dreams, or check out her latest publications, visit www.thecontentvixen.com.

www.ingramcontent.com/pod-product-compliance
Lightning Source LLC
Chambersburg PA
CBHW020125130526
44591CB00032B/524